Platform

Rodrigo Toscano

atelos

15

© 2003 by Rodrigo Toscano
ISBN 1-891190-15-6

First edition, first printing

Acknowledgments:
Some of these poems have appeared in the following periodicals: *Bombay Gin, Poetics Journal, Cross Cultural Poetics, Tripwire, Open Letter, Cello Entry, Kenning, Kenning Audio Editions, Perspektive, Slought Networks, 580 Split, Combo, The Tangent, Snare, Aufgabe, The Literary Review, The Brooklyn Rail, DC Poetry Anthology, Cities Of Chance: An Anthology of New Poetry from The United States and Brazil (Rattapallax)*, and *Crayon*. The author wishes to thank the publishers for their support and encouragement.

Cover photography and design by Dirk Rowntree

Ŧ Atelos
A Project of Hip's Road
Editors: Lyn Hejinian and Travis Ortiz

Platform

Contents

Group 1

Early Morning Prompts for Evening Takes (or, Roll 'em!)   15

Piece Beginning with Some Haunting Lines from Bertolt
    Brecht's "The Doubter"   20

Pre-Capitalist *Duende* Outbounds Archie-Dependent Kontent?
   28

Poetics   30

On a Literary Journal (Satire No. 1)   34

A Brief Retrospective of Chump De Ville's Poetic Oeuvre over
    the Last Decade (Satire No. 2)   38

My Target Audience, As It *Is* an Issue... (Satire No. 3)   43

Group 2

A Beginner's Guide to Day Trading   57

The Codes of U.S. Trade Reps, "As a Worm Weaves Silk"   63

Connectivity, Polonius, Soil Science, and You (and Your Diet)
   70

Eight Struggling Voices, Now Barely Struggling at All (An All
    Instrumental Version)   74

Group 3
In-Formational Forum Rousers—Arcing (Satire No. 4)   89

Group 4
Fourteen Superimposed Pockets of Formally Unified Subjectivity as Mass-Aggregate Social Subject, or, *Politesse Politique*, or, Monologue of The "Free Radical"   163

But Will Your Social Memory Cause Constipation Later in the Day, or That Something Else in the Morning?   167

Affekt Funereal / Affekt Jamboree   169

Ideo-Degradable Verses from Immokalee   175

Jukebox Selection, a Brick and Mortar Remembrance   181

Die Warheit Ist Konkret   184

Some Brooklyn Northside *Calaveritas* (Little Skulls) (Ironic Morsels)   187

Group 5
About the Amadou Diallo Police Shooting, a Verse Letter to T.G.   197

Blue-Green Superfund Roundelay   204

A Postscript   207

General Secretary Lula's Last Stand?	210
Notes on the Great Strike of '97	214
And Yet Another Incipient Form or Face, Venal "Left" Cooptative Rump of the WTO, NGO-ite Operative's Proclamation—Baldly—Put	218
Hidden Harvest	223
Some Thoughts on the Upcoming Quebec Summit, or Fractals from the I-Experience Colliding with the We-Experience, Utterances	228

Group 1

Early Morning Prompts for Evening Takes
Or, Roll 'em!

Like being reassigned to a case being made—to win?

>for a world
>mocked-up—terms
>to contest?

Or, *self* glutting the market of experience—

>am am, a
>did this that—
>as "voice" script?

Or, reining in the thrusting impulse that'd *burst—out!*

>and into…
>*timed* pattern
>a male's—"mine?"

Or, a hyper-local cultural thing—to do—

>conscious stance
>between friends
>strung along?

Or, some gnawing negation—impelling all this?

>din' wanna
>(really did)
>am "writing?"

Or, being dispatched to a cramped corner of the vast...

    work-a-day
    transactions
    transmission?

Or, alibis for (if not *from*) the near Black Out—

    detecting
    vital signs
    of dissent?

Or, The National—reifying itself—can read?

    preemptive
    authorships
    as "progress"?

Or, a once-elitist practice—popularized—

    aimless youth
    called forth—I
    came (aimed at?)

Or, recombinant ruses of power—"allure"—

    who writes who
    here—and how
    sex—transects?

Or, Capital's quandaries of identity—

> certified—
> the stakes—now
> lowered? raised?

Or, malingering with History's inducements—

> disciplined
> we *won't* be
> though *are*—need?

Or, a schedule of vanguardist—occupations—

> vacuum left
> by the left
> to fill out?

Or, the Nors that can't be stated (just yet) can—mean?

> forming trends
> at the base
> asserting?

Or, wouldn't non-pop perspectives be also writ?

> discursive
> bumps and grinds
> to report?

Or, logging on to a collectivizing—*chance*?

    bodies here
    plunked down—will
    plunk up…toward?

Or, newly glozed invectives—to desublimate?

    old belles lettres
    upgraded
    downplays *gain*?

Or, the pervasive *libertinage* of Genres—

    which clothes which
    strips which—for
    thrills—mostly?

Or, a progressivist (scientistic)—*complex*?

    regrounding
    the grounds (props
    dignity?

Or, an overdue reunion with *precedence*—

    compulsion
    to *just flake*
    kept in check?

Or, why *did* you come—to hear something you don't know?

>   already—
>   sorting terms—
>   assigned to?

Or, a realization of what's yet unrealized—

>   postscript or
>   preamble
>   to praxis?

Piece Beginning with Some Haunting Lines from Bertolt Brecht's "The Doubter"

"Are you in the stream of happening?
Do you accept all that develops?
Are you too ambiguous?
Each possible misunderstanding is *your* responsibility.
Are you *too unambiguous*—taking the contradictions out of things
(If so, what you say is useless. Your thing has no life in it)."

of steel—

k'

t'ain't—

k'

clamshell
particle
neither—

analog
material (k')
consistency, of
"commitment"—

        pffff...is right

(and not a highly haggled-over grapheme
"pffff")

nevertheless
        dissimulate

small-miracles
on Mott Street

in the clause
struggle—

        and justify the ways of pun
        to fun—

interceptive—
digressive—
ambulatory—

        not an ultra-magnetic
        nor slimy froggy skin
        cathexis
        —*ideal*—

but discursive cross-sections
(dzzz) flash-welded, or (dzzz) drilled out (libidinously)
then strung together with
whatever's handy

—*ideal*—

                    and that the horizon of literature
                    (world-wide) is still
                    literacy *itself*

as exeunt the 90s, 80s—
wire-cut-splice-*cast*
must
RT
ante
up or
stay
put
(putt putt) poems
empathic
vatic
ideo-doppler
detect
blustering
hot topic
anticipatory
opportunism?

"*my* ideal match," says the piece (looking for an author) "is:"

                    lowballer broker for
                    high authority
                    resistant
                    carrier

                        subjects
—Dont's: *don't*
        de-materialize me, author—

—Do's: *gotta*
        re-materialize me, author—

...and that's the way we understood
catapult splayed-ego
foco-istas in the mist
praxis
back when...

        regrets?
        few—

the anti-belletristic
aesthetic decoy relays
were
post-instrumentalist
intra muros
banter
anyway

a round of
mercenary althusserianisms
playing back

30 (or thereabouts) *neue*
amerikanische
dichter

slogged—
logged in

riffed on what
langpos done
did
deconstitutively

(later I
labor-ite
overlay)

"j'ai une question—

(they'll say
pugilist detractor
rearguard)

"how do old surds
like you
find room enough

to grub about
the psychic lots—abondonné

in the wireless century?"

(and)

"comme tu...
comp to
so charged
a goal
abolir, la column!
ideal of

social reconstitution? "

but whoa!
—wireless wunderkind—

fakey, *charro*, as in
artista (disque "dialogista" civíl) *charro*

(corporativista hijo de su—)

         "that's a spry strophe
         you got there
         sonny"

    "that's a gnarly scar
    you got there
    gramps"

k'

k'

all the while the piece (k')
(piece again here reeling)
cannot be
periodized
enough"

      and that the horizon of literature
      (world-wide) is still
      literacy *itself*

(for women, especially)

"*so*—
he's *soo*
prescriptive!"

 'kay—

k'

add, one Roque Dalton, melted, splashed unevenly onto
four slabs of modernist-steel, encased in see-thru lit-critical
polymer, flecked with two pounds of dialectical-clamshell
flakes—

add, a few strips of pomo-silk wrapped loosely around her
neck—Alexandra's, that is (Kollontai)—one bust (clean shaven),
on a (two foot) platform, covered in papier-mâché of
3-line poems, all penned in
sweatshop conditions
tongue agape
atop it all—

        this sculpture
        is called
        "Commitment No. 2"

        "No. 1" has been
        sold (out)

        "Commitment No. 3"
        is now
        under construction

Pre-Capitalist *Duende* Outbounds Archie-Dependent Kontent?

"el sol brillante
se apaga
de repente

*y de repente
me arrepiento*"

what the Bard spat forth, sublimates

the Michoacan "profe"

*as hereto unknown levels of
paranoiac
mexi-global
minstrelsy
take firm hold of The Old Literary Quartet
(in the bar)
they interrupt one another
in jaunty rhythms—*

(rough translation)

"*ill* what would be me will-pile—file—*sing*"

"stuff up what would be blind-fuck there—spare, me, hope's hope"

"*I* the devil what would more design
trans-death, than trans-life"

"call in the faith box— that would be premise
dream-lense, be-shattered,
shyshtemic
shubsherviensh"

And so the Declamatory session ends.

Bottles are cleared from the table.

And a last *fleur
de malaise globale*

is plucked

"Rue the monograph!

but not the ineluctable *practice*

young man"

Symbolism's
satellite
debris

Poetics

Pyongyang, if you'll *please*, STOP
                         appearing
                         in the poem
like this—
unannounced

*

In writing to your
Pomomomo

(that special critical *topos*
between an ideolophe *fahtha'*
and a para-juridical *muhtha'*)

This-side-of-the-Hudson
Psycho-Acoustics

Jangling—

Claim you
what?

"We call it dead in the *wa wa*
don' mean *jacky bits*"

"Pyongyang"

*

But it *does*...
as an In Walk Bud
flips the *whooole* session
on its head

lexicals
in range
clash
and dash out

patch 14ths
off the scale
to perfect fifths
effects

REACT
rather more *differently*
than before

with
"Pyongyang"
in there

*

And "Quetzalcoatl"

lands on
"Tarragon"

jangling it?

If *that's* where the Nitro's stored, in
"Tarragon"

bird's *already* been
blown off

feathers
falling

field's been
re-charged

*

And "Thatcher?" as guest
jaw-harp
soloist?

the E.U.'s
formative
contradictions

unresolved?

some *kill* in *that* cut—

you got the mic, *pomomomo*

make a ho' youself

and Maggy

and us

On a Literary Journal (Satire No. 1)

for the bare bones crew

Galleries of imagistic (neo-immanantist) "insides" as
(had to—gotta be?) Conduit—for: *intrinsic* (historically
    operative) *logic*
deconstitutive logic—Capital's: extrinsic cultural foyers—
    abstractions—higher and higher

("mentations," they called them, in the 19th century)

(said)
       logic
boring—
       into
existing
       linguistic structures

[equal—at base, those (logic, structure)—but the offsetness, the
trans- (or be it intra-) *real*
      Estrangement   Engagement
                           prattle
                           content

               undialogically
               rendered
"communities" of
"descriptions" and
complimentary encryptionists (authors)

                        productive

                  * proto-national affinities *
→ *an' do it do dat?*

                Censor
(in minimalist or expansivist mode)

→ *it do!*

—through   <u>the pervasive</u>

            Shut-It-All-Out (titude)

gallery-time dream of, clean canvasses of, unused space of
                              —readily available—*acumen?*

(some note the *demographical achievement* precedes the front)

of
pervasive (has to—gots to be?) lexically

                  <u>abstentionist</u>

           Shut-It-All
                -Out (titude)
inverted *socio-scapes,* starring
"absence" (Modernesque kook) and cousins
            "Being *itself*" and Being as, everything else
                                      remaining
of which—
      Post-Langpo (and dismissive of it) inscriptionist

mannerism

[thanks for the useful moniker Louis (Cabri)]

                       (yes) neo-mannerist
proh-ject

        foregrounds the
                      ANTI-EXPRESSIONISM

[socio-causal *expression*, in the Lukácsian sense, to rally to—anew?
                   bumps up—against two...efforts]

         likened here as
corkscrew shavings
         likened here as
                having been
bored
out
of
   existing   don't so much as *dicker* with—(status quo)
                Material Relations

                h o m o l o g i c

mentations, as in
"to mentate"
mentators!

likened here as
             gathered up
             reparticalized

                              proto-anthological
                                         poetic
(uh huh)   *matériel*
"corkscrew
       shavings"

(core, or
coöpted)
       personnel

       in the process of   *R*egroup

       in the process of

(end-around) neo-mannerist
                (moderno) (dogmato) retro-empirico
                                         gringectial
                                         inscriptionism

put to—and
quite up to—the
(Historical) task

                       (*to* their credit)

                       current

                       Current

A Brief Retrospective of Chump DeVille's Poetic Oeuvre over the Last Decade (Satire No. 2)

...raised to <u>principle</u> [but *never* to put it quite like *that*]

                                      is
                               REACTIVE

to the Social –

jump! fetch! roll!
                left! right!
                          right! right!

"responsive" calls it ?
"I do *respond* to it all—as ever, and *re-*
[key prefix, by which to spot'em, in any room] *re-*
figure it – it [recycle bins full of] is

                        certifiable
                                 "PROVISIONAL"

...term, so bleached of its original color—so cleaved of its urgent
    pairing, *praxis*

                    (an organizational *praxis*)

But CV, knowing where the goods are, goes there:

The official [now academicized] site of
provisionality, click here for

Quietistic
"rigor"

"...As when Bands
Of Pioneers with Spade and Pickax arm'd
Forerun the Royal Camp, to trench a Field,
Or cast a Rampart"

[that is, from one conference to another]

But just how <u>competitive</u> *is* Chump
De Ville?

At the Turn of the Millennium:
N30, A16, S26 / and counting –

And just how current *are* his maps
drawn up, rolled out, pointing the way out
                                                to
positional
positionality? (2nd patristic term)
in the castle, or just outside, the castle...

"The serpents sly in trailing forward stirred
so softly you would have thought they still asleep had been"

And gearing up, proceeds, though, *in reverse*:

Tactics first, Strategy second, Theory third

—after that, a *consolidation*
of a sort of "base," an IDIOM
is to be established

and diversified
    and liquidated
        and redeployed

"provisional"

At the Turn of the Millennium

his generation (same as mine, a Reagan Teen)
while another—at his heels nips, is
stone-to-the-bone activist

strategic along
    representational lines...

And Chump, in charge also of channeling what's not properly
  pliant ("contingent")
—and who's not compliant with The Order's prescripts—and
  maps it, accordingly—
balks at the suggestion of his *own* "fixity" (3rd patristic term)

"oh to vex mee, contraries meete in one:
Inconstancy unnaturally hath begot
A constant habit; that when I would not
I change in vows, and in devotion."

40

And nows
                    what's called for is
(drum roll)

                    A *linking?*
of 'em!

a "coalition" of such
circles

shall be unspoken –
pre-programmatic
                    post-politically aligned

Paratactic Methodism?

                    Metaphoric Judaism?

Metonymic Pentecostalism?

                    Figurative Catholicism?

Non-Representational Atheism?

                    Literal Agnosticism?

Ok, all.

But still,

R E A C T I V E

Lines in quotes from the following, respectively: Milton's *Paradise Lost*, Book One; Golding's translation of Ovid's *Metamorphoses*, Book Seven; Donne's *Divine Meditations*.

My Target Audience, As It *Is* an Issue... (Satire No. 3)

is much like fresh gum stuck on yr. pant leg
from under a lounge booth
upon just arriving—
wearing new pants—
you can't afford
anyway

        to be party to, or declaim, or resist—

ALL THOSE OVERDETERMINED SOAPBOX CRATES

(brought up from under the dry critical cellar, encasing now
ethically sour wines, to be drunk by demoralized re-moralizing
drunkards!)

        and these, paired with

ALL THOSE UNDERDETERMINED COINAGES

(jinglings in yr. pockets, curious-to-look-at transport tokens
from far-flung metropoles—or futures,
one residing there (or not)
or wishing to (or not))

...that it's *sticky*, Fidelius, a non-unified
target audience
a *split* audience

—though, it's what confronts us squarely, and
main reason for which
I write

lexically alert
to controvert
the pathetic

syntactically de-obviate
to re-translate
the pathetic

enforced
systemic
specifications

...molds us into
polymer clay figurines...

- high insulation capability
- fully thermo-elastic (can be reprocessed numerous times)
- abrasion resistant
- high-impact resistant
- colorable, printable
- at some grades, biocompatible

I, "elitist!"
      "non-optimist!"

since you style me so—

I, now
without imprimatur of

          people's pep talk
          poetics
          phrenologizing
          "depth"

          of engagement

          "aaah…*there's* a doozy!"

water-witching for

near-the-surface wits
on Fridays—

and so, yes, *my* audience

      will get smaller
      as it gets broader

      while yours, larger
      as it gets narrower

* * *

I will, however, strive to maintain relations
with the following:

    Teleo-territorial
    assets
    protectors

    Stark motha' nekid
    re-vocalizing

hope
lyricizers
Ideologeme gem
polishing
trafficking
ring
leaders

Transubstantiatory Keynesian
retro-incrementalist
"revolutionist"
(and by reverse-default!)
truculent
literary
gladiators

Ancillaries to no pomo-left rising
tough angling yet
medium-soft talk
o, inside, more lettuce
than meat
men,
and women—

…if that's "formalism" to you, Fidelius,
then this too is
formalistically

optimal

in that
it addresses
your distress

(—and *this* irony, *you've* sparked
into consciousness)

        being a splinter
        of a splinter
        of a splinter

        of the audience

* * *

But what's this now? you grimace?
you don't expect that I expect—you
to make a more *efficient*

        high-density literalide infusion

process *case*

against a poly-foyerous struggla-cide
rapid-separation
process

of The National
Expectation?

non-unifying
signifying-practices
emissions
not stirring in you
an appetite for them?

your
(index 100 log)
"t'aint fer notins"

—but wait!

(and Dante, if you might again, please)

"And just as he who, with exhausted breath,
having escaped from sea to shore, turns back
to watch the dangerous waters he has quit..."

your future panting

(as might mine—historically)

in gum-stuck stasis of
over-performed
near-censure of

power relations—

you'd agree—
(index 200 log)
"fer sometins"

    …are they to be packed with paleo-moral ice to freeze—off? or cut out, and later ideo-pragmatically patched over? or pulled clear off   *now*

—*throw your pants out!*

huh
    huh

       huh
huh—

(into the crowd)

…better to err on the side of
worker tough nuts enlightenment, I'd still say—

than
imprimatur-ship of

>people's pep talk
>poetics
>phrenologizing
>"depth"
>
>of engagement
>
>"aaah…*there's* a doozy!"

water-witching for
near-the-surface wits
on Saturdays

*   *   *

Alack,
what a conflicted relief it gives me

>your standing back

       from the edge
       of the platform

"we're serious about peril
your peril"

            sated

macadamia

Group 2

A Beginner's Guide to Day Trading

pre-
scared
as czech's
said of
busting
a move
on it
the regime

—

full of
found
harking options
bigger than
bite's
growl
growth rates
baits

—

goal?
a bank
with a fund
a john

to a pimp
your cut's
my fee
dual plunderocracy

—

industry / labor
side
agreements
stack the board
with market
dominance
festooned as
mutual providence

—

I thought
I thaw
a trade pact cat
rat
in its paws
literal-impact
fact-death
yelps

—

well *you've* got some verve!
to swerve
around
a hound
of bloody
sanction in the night
default setting
gang

—

bored?
uncage
a filial osprey
co-nato-ite
blairified
transatlan
-frantical
unfuckingrightgaggable

—

who be dead pan?
'round here
asks heraclitus
freed us
from
democritus'
orderly atoms?

pakistan

—

thief
I do believe
this was yours
not a year ago
for the price now of
one-half florin anthrax wine
join me
proto-stately

—

'sta cabrón
plunging corn
index
in
zaca-cejas
deregulasonic
bust boom
histrionic

—

give!
me!

my!
value!
I don' care
what I said!
the client state
to the clientele

—

telecom
-mune
-ism
fibers
of the world
ignite!
liberal schliberal
front

—

chuh' chuh'
chaiii
-na!
the pace is strange
chuh' chuh'
chaaina
jus' tryin' da' find a
funda'

—

of course not
not forgot
what it's wrought
likkud
who could
with shas
exacerbate hamas
re-tally yr. stock's loss

The Codes of U.S. Trade Reps—
"As a Worm Weaves Silk"

Malaysia

kick start

casting couch

delegation

Barshefsky

socks in the mouth

athletic

platform

toggler

aceptémos

these rules on trade

☼

"when Anu the Sublime, King of the Anunaki, lord of Heaven and Earth decreed the fate of the land, and assigned to Marduk, dominion over earthly man,
and made him great among the Igigi..."

☼

will *probably*

force borrowing costs, watch for signs of

insurrection

deflate wages

to target rate

"these international liaison types"

"an open question still, which—" says Sung Won Sohn,
of Wells Fargo (Minneapolis)

"hasn't been put to bed, quite yet"

☼

the experimental-poetry scene

has not shifted (unexpectedly)

to Minneapolis

☼

"so that they (the Igigi) should rule over the black-haired people like Shamash, and enlighten the land, to further the well-being of mankind?"

Code 274 (of 282)

—274: If any one hire a skilled artizan, he shall pay as wages of the ... [fragmented, missing text] *five gerahs*, as wages of the potter *five* gerahs, of a tailor *five* gerahs, of ... gerahs, ... of a ropemaker *four* gerahs, of ... gerahs, of a mason ... gerahs ... per day

☼

some *gestalt analyst* you

some *elevated temporary dismissal* you

some *falling demand* you

some *concentrated response* you

some *dissipated warning* you

some *overheated speculator* you

☼

"We'd expect a noticeably milder investment climate,'" says David Orr, chief economist at First Union Corp. (Charlotte)

[a volcano of experimentalism—Charlotte]

☼

some dealers

expect a more neutral poesy

taking a less acidic partisan tone

☼

"demand may be moderating"

"demand *has* moderated!"

a change in verb tense

expectation

☼

"some just wait to see how things evolve" says Mr. Hammurabi, president of Future View Relations TLC (Cleveland)

suburb of Pepper Pike, Ohio

borough of Uzbekistan

☼

jabs & dodges

transcaucusoid policy

oil lines

and yr. lines

in good stead?

echo Malaysia skeptics

opec output

trans-siphonoid

nasturtium in the mouth

bathetic

forum

barter

am we

Seattlelitic

for years to come?

☼

Barshefsky—behind closed doors

"chances are *slim* for

setting a new agenda"

"more standoff positions on *all* issues"

☼

BABYLON, N-Y-C

☼

a series of

supply lines

planned demand

a series of

reading series

☼

TRANSAMERICA, S-F

☼

"so that they should rule over the black-haired people like Shamash, and enlighten the land, to further the well-being of mankind?"

Code 282 (this being the last of 'em)

"If a slave say to his master: "You are *not* my master," if they convict him, his master shall cut off his ear"

☼

"I don't have much of an ear

for that kind of poetry"

is what they say

still

in Dayton

☼

(right)

Connectivity, Polonius, Soil Science, and You (and Your Diet)

Digidestined
wagons
gleam
by

am
-biently

creaking
private
freedoms
forms?

or flaggèd norms
souped-up
bossonomic
expansive(ly)
intrusive

Irrational Authority, *Irrational* Production,
$\qquad\qquad\qquad\qquad\qquad$ Distribution, Consumption—

Swipe the grin (and cut)
that cheeky chimp's
$\qquad\qquad\quad$ "new agency's"
optimism—

wits—

and paste
onto
"just crumbs" doc.

who "gets"
it

A discrete sector's
and chiefly *that* discrete sector's
     cultural terrain
        extolled

storied—
and, miraculously (that is, by inversions) "*peopled*"
and attired in
   tight-fitting

   fibs

* * *

[*enter Polonius*]

..."*emergent* civic" (emergent Prince), it is my exclusive honor
and rather morose pleasure, to introduce to you "*residual* civic,"
who is now visiting us (as rump populations are wont to do)
from Lansing, Michigan; whereon his daughter's received and

treasured forms of freedom (dialectically all wrought, and not
all with conspicuous lack of conspicuous grace)
are being *disciplined*— here, at
(Elsinore) NYU department of

MULTIMEDIA

(a bargaining unit
in the making, I should add, sire—)

...wha'?
and, "and *lose* the name of *action*?"

abandoned to collusive and censorious, non-extrapolative
                                                                reportage?
no, sire, to die *not*,
but to live, *to live*, TO LIVE!

in the interstices of
global
agribusiness

crumbs

...is verily more wealth-stealthy, more stealth-wealthy

"baaaaahteri wan' dolla'"

than the more foppish co-determinous *sectors*
                              (Fortune-Brash 500, S & P's)

—so, to aspire, sire

to some spire
in the city
and *not* perspire

"baaaaahteri wan' dolla"

is sweetest sweat and dislocation

—not scheisse, m'lord—not scheisse—

raining down

on us—

ethical flimflam to wade through (nay to concoct—invert, *and* broadcast)

but *hearth*! profit!
only—

translated into ALL languages!

but lo!
spokes of the off-shore wheel
(of fortune)

the poets—they come!

mono-meta-thesis!
intra-intellect-catharsis
antithesis ho!

Eight Struggling Voices, Now Barely Struggling at All (An All Instrumental Version)
4-2001

1. High-definition suck-up (luck)

equipped with
special sounds
and standardized emoticons
for *special* assignments

the plug-and-play resource
exclaims,

"I'll make a *great* Guy Monday! Wait and see"

"I won't be *degraded*
by your upgraded downgrading of my language-applications
that often! Wait and see"

"I'm same-day
cooptation
guaranteed!
Wait and see"

*alright alright, and that you grew up on a commune's
what's coming next, isn't it?
how attuned, and so forth—*

we're sorry—

you don't seem to possess a certain...

I-can I-can I-can
(hack)

all-day
      frontal
      strapped on
      gortex
      gag-ball

reality

2. The prez's press secretary meets the press

"...if you might define 'presidential firewall'?"

a security stool
to protect
against
packers

"and if the press abroad, say that of Inner Europa
dissents, or can't come to terms with the AOL TIME-WARNER
version of events—ours?"

then, the firewall, of course
—thank you, that'll be all—

the nymphs
are departed

*

adelante—

contenido escondido

mic-stand solo

fusiles

descarga fatal

3. The "bi-partisan" wing nut—tightened—on the turret hatch—of the tank—of the session—of the house—of the field of—operations, speaks—

"at the first level of visual titillation

(the images on yr. screen)
my head (purposeful)
is denied a purpose
having more than a flirtatious cross-purpose
or license (both *never* questioned)
(a relied-upon misalignment) and
transcending-the-individual-ego *possibly*
but more likely, that is to say

the transparency wig
changes position on different faces
(see here how it lopes over my purposeful brow just so)
so that the wig itself, also changes to individual positions
of the head—

so, wig first, then face, then words—

word-of-mouth wise I tell you, my Fellow Americans

my private parts have less patience for
tracing the lines of material causality back to an exploitative
Gemeinschaftlichkeit
than

the most broken-down of you has

a passion
for pass-or-fail
education

to restore respect

for full bore
devolution

of social provision"

4. "*Shit* I be working *for* Baghdad!" the lively poet said—at a slam-abad. I listened and imagined him being slapped with the corresponding charges.

Clinton Legacy:
The 1996 anti-terrorist laws (Reno)
drastically (and vaguely) cast a net over dissenters (language)
in times of "operations"
(that's every other day)

So that sulking over Ashcroft (on that account)

would be in a continuum

Funny, we're not hearing it that way from our liberal

always-already "political"

writers

5. The shrunken shrink shirks at consciousness-forming, yet

"which image
pops up first, upon hearing:

'palette'

mhm...mhm...mhm...

and *'Parks'?*

mhm...

what about *'Dreyfus'?*

Alfred
or Richard?

Ah, Richard *for* Alfred

mhm...

well, I think we might begin by
dosing you with

contra-factoids masticatables

starting with...

Nellie Bly's
exposé on mental institutions

(a muckraker groundbreaker) of 1890

...still a shoulder holster
(if can you image *that*, a shoulder holster)
for *our* side

of The Argument

PROGRESS

and Zola,
a pocket watch

(if you can image *that*)

and Robeson,

a palm pilot"

6. The human-kind ideologically-intolerant-to-*itself*, speaks (without a teleprompter!)

"an epoxy class?
what?

pulverized consciousness?

into a dust?

—hosed down, soaked?
and turbine-mixed?
into an epoxy?
class?

spackled?
into crevices?

welding together granite
capitalist
advancements?

that I am
this very night

monumentally

autotoxicly

a *champ*

'we are the champions' nonetheless

of the season?

is that the reason
the I-Beams of the subway on my way to work
though cold, inanimate, and repetitive,
speak to me?

*'this is
what I am'*

'what art thou?'

Ha! you can't entreat me to jump on the tracks just yet!
I-Beam, because I'm not edifying you
just now, with

barely intelligible
broken character witness

poetry

—I've a train to catch!"

7. Notes on the Great Aromatherapeutic REVOLT of '98

uh-*huh*...

8. For my mother's Catholic circle of friends

the host speaks:

"As an F14-penetrated *faminist*, I hereby, however, do *not* sanction the introduction of

the pope in a condom costume
—ham hock in a *suave* sock—

as the soiled reliquary
of the season—

as on a runway
of a carrier, a fashionable
appearance
praying for peace

though these times *do* demand
piety! mixed with
dash!

as in a
Romanza Policiaca
(picante)

(*rap beats*) ♪ ♪

"christians all *hyped up*
if the muslims *rise up*
we ain't gettin' *showed up*"

♫ ♫

(go pope go pope)

♫ ♫

"bodies all *chopped up*
when the bodies *pop up*
I ain't gettin' *locked up*"

♫ ♫

(go pope go pope)

♫ ♫

GO TA BAGHDAD! (tsh)
GO TA BAGHDAD! (tsh)
GO TA BAGHDAD! (tsh)

grab that bag that booty up   back-it-up back-it-up back-it-up

popa packa   packa popa   popa packa

♫ ♫

(he's a meshuggana!)

♫ ♫

(es el Diablo!)

♫ ♫

"a spiritual dimension is needed for every conquest of capitalist liberty"

Group 3

In-Formational Forum Rousers—Arcing (Satire No. 4)

A small
American Town
large mall
horniness

a poetry *sub*scene's
objects

laid bare

—a shoplifting spree

deep inside you

a never know how to quite get you some
(fractured) disquisition
on

(horizontal) desiring
structures?

arrive in the mail—

(yearly subscriptions actually)

—cultural-capital *angling*

(that's "dangling," without the 'd')

affordability

—pollo loco—

bi-national franchise

gone *tri*—

peripatetic perkforce

twerkers

lateraturizations

you don't need to know but he'll tell you anyway

"you hot roll'em like this (and make sure your Sanico hat's on snug—always, the paper one—over your head) then you wrap 'em up like this...then ding the bell"

<habitus?>

*

Barfidicus Pragmaticus The Elder
To Barfidicus The Younger

"The *satura*, Barfy
needn't come to a full stop

before eliciting
several hearty
snorts"

"*but I see
my job-failure
in my poetry-family's eyes
already*"

"that's
structuo-reflexo-simpatico of you
that's

subltedistinctionpsychlike"

<habitus?>

*

Heuristic
medium-range
epistle

post-humanistic
pre-arch-globotic

agentic—

strays
off course
(of course)

the *design* of it
intends to

disable

The Intra-
National
Creative
Bedroom
Privacy
Act

of 2000 ... *when?*

<click>

"guarantees—
yr. textual
freedom-seeking
procedures
lock in on—"

<click>

shout outs to:
'futural intersubjectivites'
"summoning"

what? (if they ask, indecorously)

"Current
Mutt-Ethereal
Relations"

*4% of the world, the U.S.
expends
25% of the resources*

('in-calls only'

International?)

*

"He's an *old* 'Centrist'
you'd love him!

we have to get you two <screwed> together...somehow"

flush—
sheetrock to plaster

"is this a false wall?
or a *real* wall?"

(knock knock
knock)

<*habitus?*>

*

<initialize new session within
current session>

<patch in:
single-hulled track of the
"Exxon Valdez">

<66 syllables to *ping* only *one*
ideologeme
resonator?>

<test it>

"Captain Hazlewood (no Faust he)
runs aground on Bligh Reef"

<go on>

"howling winds
buffet his .06 b.a.c.
(cross-cut surface)
face"

<cut out "cross-cut surface"—obvious wink
to artworld
savvy>

"sentenced—
to scoop up
<pause—causality check: patch in
it was only a pint and a half
two hours previous> roadside litter
for five years"

<ready? *launch*—"the resonator">

"But, <u>systemically</u> speaking, it was a <u>systemic</u>
<u>system</u> of safety
<u>system</u> failure"

<okay? *okay*—now fade>

"…it's not just *one* cause, but a *complex* of *root* causes
that leads to the
'TOP' event—"

<ok, it's *out* there—now cut>

This is—
an admittedly *horizontal* scheme
in an *admittedly* <agh—no, cut it, cut it now> <u>vertical</u>
'socio' 'power' 'scape'

Vertical idealist gnosis—"company pukes"

This training's
spillings—such that

committee's recommendation is

<com-recommem *who?*>

1. Back up (cheap) alarms be put on deck (Vulgar Formalism)

2. Sea lanes be monitored continuously by *commissioned* watchman (Vulgar Realism)

<*you!* die hard
dialec->

"and a double-hulled

paranational (unsutured) subjectivity

can (but certainly not of its *own* strength)

design out the cause—"

<*now* you've *stoked* it!>

"stroked

who?"

*

Nor-(Ouija)
Board
Consultation

BLODIG: En blødende demonstrant blir fjernet av italiensk sikkerthetspoliti under opptøyene i Genova.

BLOODY: (embloodied demonstrator) (removed becomes) (by) (Italian Security Police)

*

Trump-O-Saurus
-Hex
crane
rearing

in blasted out
green granite
ditch

94th and Lex

iglesias
unisex
complex

done booted out—hallelujah'd
out of

Community Board *Bribe* $

['Shift+4'

dollar-sign keystroke

techfactoid

incidental

pushup pop—poet

roll out

barrels of

purah—

jk' jk' jk'—*ks'*]

Independent Candidacy
out of Brooklyn
cost 20 [nice rounded figure]
connubial crackups

index: *economie triangulaire*

several slopes downward

"options"

over-inherited wealth

options

yearly—

and the antiphonal
public of Ken Burns'
origins myths

a Dutch
of a diddling
imagination's

private access
statuementary

—oh, and the adjunct
retro-barrio
sunset <collegiate>
poetry troop

on tour—

—oh, and the Vulgar Formalist gaming center

—each sign includes a consonant, a vowel, and a
—hotdiggity! *portside!* (check'em out)

purpose

leaping

makes

historicity
splash

still epistemic

foam

<habitue?>

*

And a *wie gehts* to you
with a tangled parachute
companion
chapbook

Where does *my* inspiration go?

Landfills in Pennsylvania
Incinerator in Newark
Incinerator in Hamstead

Unpaid work in exchange for

a little water, stiffened with flour, in imitation of a shoemaker's paste

hard food, poor lodgings, confused dialection, *fatigue*—
the trapezoidal-faced pimp-n-ho' of Essex County's part of it—

The Can't Endure—

What sweet felicities have I left at home!

Barges

lift lid, extend wrist, and drop—

That is the end of this line

*

<re-initialize
'Satire No. 4'
"from here">

<increase
social base
memory
buffer>

<thank who?>

BERSERK: En maskert anti-kapitalist sparker inn et vindu i en butikk i Genovas gater.

BERSERK: (one masked) (anti-capitalist) (kicks in) (a window) (of one) (boutique) (in Genova's streets)

Conglomerate   Transatlantic   Pantocracy

"philosophy"

psank u
poor
prefoosening
ox & axy swung
a-flexti
ranger
traded
"furd"
gen
"u"
fleck
stirr at
carbono
familiex
grouppe

grazi

cough & wheeze

teary eye'd

"chaunge"

[come again?]

"chaunge the chaunnel"

tear gas canister
whirling
on five-century-old
laid-in-stone
alley

green-glow & pink-glow

chalk

chalked in
slogans

blurry

scuffling feet

hold steady
altered
context

lines—

crossing 'em—

[if isolate

translates to danger]

"*operazione
liberazione*

perpetua

signiore"

pata—

fisticuffs?

nyet—

something qualitatively
elser

apparently
someoner

in switch-packeted
transit
rescrambled

screen view

———

Ron Phillyman
on a Bart somewhere

can't help—
can't re-particulate me (who?)
me me me—

"now now now"

pot banging!
pot banging!

(echo)

Buzzards
hover a long-picked-over <victorian> Novel

Naturalism's
inverted—carcass
fleshless

not all's *that* safari-like
no more

for the demo
outfitted

pantaloons
safety-pinned
ludicrous
we, only

hybridity
focus!—in the cross hairs

'indentity?'

Artiste

Après tout!

how ever
did

thniggle thnaggle thnuggle

at ("upgrade now!")

barriers—

warning:
conflicting run-time race politics drivers
delete?

("*une gauche* gauche, eh?")

gosh—
Barfy—
I don' see any fledgling literati in the
(immaterially-labored)
grass

grazing on…

blots

"huh?"

blots

STEINKASTING: Tildekte demonstranter kaster stein mot politiet.

———

fund   a

mental

ism—
schism

recruitment?

in snatches?

I wonder

(Alpha) Spanner, why not *dual* inducement?

Formal *and* Programmatic

fajita fave
recipes
flavors

bundled with

fajita-maker
relative
clock-rate

throughput

value

calibrated—

"and then ding the bell"

dynamics

(more on this later)

*

Psss—

it's docked, it's unloaded
cultural
cargo

Psst!

kris kringle
a gift economy
scab

Pss—

capacity to the <u>max</u>
papi

Pss—

I don' know nob*ah*dee,
I don' know nob*ah*dee here

Pst!

the department chair
is against
the union, *man*

Pss—
so are *you*!
gaawd—

Pss—

this reading *sucks!*
(sucks!)

Pss—

DUMBO
has come back to life
they say
in

L.A. County
(proper)

Five Curators

(one, a Latrino—serviceable)

"we feature *individual* success here
not a cobra pit of
paranational
minor literature
tail up (ending)
(busting)

expat
pariahships"

———

The Secret Password?

"cake"

(*every* global girl and boy wants…)

<thank you>

blots

<*habitus?*>

*

*The Top 1%
in the United States
has amassed over
40% of the nations wealth*

("clarify")

spank dem
goor
ptrewoosening
oz & azy dwung
a-yexti
langer
mraded
"purd"
ven
"b"
cleck
purr at
droganus
familiex
grouppe

*

When that a schiksa
with a muckraker huckster
was a poker-faced *spotter*
to re-certify

excrementalist poestry?

While that a popeye optimo
galvanized
newer literary
formations

contra-
servatoidal
telescopic
(dome)

a gentler
händler
web stalk
sweep
of its
(own?)
malingular
post
de-centered
boozwah
(imploded national)
(or half a half borough wide)
subject
job—

design

"did he say-

VANDALISERING: To demonstranter forsøker å ødelegge en minibank.

resign?

(VANDALISING): (two demonstrators) (attempt to try [or is it?] try to attempt) (same) (*destroy*) (an atm)"

"not the least *upended*
by my institotalization"

("I believe you"—*fideism*)

button down bobo banes, meanwhile, wants to know
what does
safado mean?

"cut loose"   "unmoored"

"de-klopted"

hvorfor?

*

"haa-*d'ya*—

[heeere he comes!]

ha-*d'ya*—

git the class struggle *in* thea'?"

[liminal gods of lit-crit protocol—he employs thee]

"Ha-*d'ya*—
git the line a' march
marchin'?"

Sorbitol-coated journal
even *with* Bourdieuean hindsight
in-con-clu-sive

Xando Café, NYC, $2.35 / cup,
40% of minimum wage

not *much* of "a living from it" (J.D.)
but a lot of—as we used to say

—out on the beaches of "hotel terminus"
the west

gankage

design a fine shine (they do)
for betta meta *bump up*?

*

But suffuse fall to winter <poet>
Roving (alley) <poet>

seen through woolly woolly folds
"scenes" as mold (spores) <poet>

cell apparatus walks a talk a stumbling into

strrrranger!

"shining"

from around

the corner <poet>

"cool"
as
"air"
as
"orange"

"leaf"

"falls"

(*leaves* fall)　(leaves *fall*)

taxi
blinks

roof

lamp

numerall'd wall—you live in

bricks

there

cool

dated

but ever new, *boet*

———

hhholiday

suffused green to its smell of
pine

war-besotted psych—
implicate
support (default)

of no *positive*
program
(as yet)

ssscatter—

<poet>

leaves

(Meiksins Wood
bereaves)

—punctuate yap ups, 'mine'

"give"

trains you've missed—
(industrial-democratic)

a heads up on—
(communicative-affective)

*jagged jagged jagged jagged
jagged*
edge of

JUSTICE

(dot) 'o' 'r' 'g'

"why—

where's that sizzling hunk of a—"

"*ovah dea*"

(humanist liberal subject?)

right
deal'

The Dis—
cord

of—

BLODIG: En blødende demonstrant blir fjernet av italiensk sikkerthetspoliti under opptøyene i Genova.

That pre-frigged Con-

—*nyet*

affix factoid on U.S. constitutive base
within IMF
—25%

All atomized mushroomy multitudes
to the great de-centered
re-centered
convergence?

"your
tempeh
'paralogical'

iguana
dinner

sir"

An empty-categoric
mimeo-syndicalist
stroblight's
on high
(just for you)
Ellen

"yr.
banana'd

flaming

Hardt and Negri
-gasmic

surprise

sir"

Blinded by the flames, polypolarized
facing
pop up
Emperium?

Please direct us to the upward-winding spiraled stairs

What stars?

(on this "occidental" rooftop)

Where orient?

Back *forward* back back *forward*

Into the—

—*fie fo fum* of it!

Foyers
Representational
Interlocking
Parts—

or,
'FRIP'

(hell, cross-platform

roles

(not the ones you over butter—

every time))

———

socialist eye-liners
winking

at ya'—

"hi ho!—it's—
con-
-tent
-o"

"*maybe,* Happy, *maybe,* there's
a role

just for you (and your six other *Ids*)
in this

move
(pent)
meant
(spent)

*

   *

* ACID MIST *

 *
*

SIRENS * *

* *

*   *

CONFUSION *

    *

*
  *

kpans med
roog
strewoopening
odd & wazy dwung
a-texty
gangler
draded
"durp"
nev
"n"
cleck
rupp at
grodanus
familiex
grouppe

Steeple top barely visible—

Santo Catzo

in the holding pen—

a rather gruff bloke

of about 80 (going on 20)

"Luxembourg…foretold the fold
of finance
by its
own
weight"

"presaged it

The Moor

like that"

<get me—

(*who?*)

mine mine mine

arse

outta here>

blots

—huh?

"*triple*

blots"

*

what hempen home-spuns have we swaggering here?

SPIES—

from the "other"
'*sub*—

scene'

contra-
dictory

problem
addicts

sub—
snub—rub-a-dub *club*
canonic

smoke devices—

on standby—

"This Doxa
is fireproof"

"you're my hero"

"code you
the flying squirrel, and thus
crack (value-added) nuts

on cue"

"An Ivy League woodchuck's
latent order to
chompity chomp
stomp—

out

openly
syndicalist poetics

on cue"

———

Compute
Gotham
Esprit
Out of the Bat Cave
Broadside

Decorative doily show

—Roll with the doilies!

(Roll—
with the Hard Facts, *sister*)

"*Cyclops*, eh?

(tonight)

such

REALISME SOCIALE!!"

<password not accepted>

"Cyclops 2"

<enter>

<skip intro>

Counterchance Operation's
Hohenpriester's Den—

banner reads:

why
affix
agitprop
decal
in toilet
stall
for *all*
to read?

"grafomaniaco"

<<cap blast>> [false alarm]

<clicker>

There's
dimensions of *un*popular front
to us all?

Frontload this with a Universalist Moral Ending (*in* the title)

"too late"

dragonsito

up—
through—
out the nose
out the high rise
window

An isolated Neo-Lukàcsian *knows* his place in the world
out the window—face—shoved—jolly: *elocutio*

Dangling—
that's cultural *angling, with* the 'd'

"tonight's readers are:

'The Democratic Text'
and
'The Plutocratic Context'"

("this oughtta be a
romper")

<*habitus?*>

*

McDonald's
playpen
determinacies
to roll around in
plasticky
frisky
games—

"cop a feel—cop a

categorical feel

in there"

("ha—dy'a"—*shush* up—)

bus rolls up, four classical idealist categories board

one gets off

—pop quiz:

how many Historically *spent* Categories

know
when to

get off—

And before she got forcibly transferred
to municipal *jail*—she said—after *him* denying *her* the good-as-cash disbursement

for a good-as-drugs *fix*

"I hay-*chu* Ronrico!"

and that's the non-trans-historicity of language
for you

digi-cams, electro-locks, laso-alarms
and a representative

payee

*

Cyclops

REALISMUS
(socialitzer)

A declaration of
autono-inter-determino

comprendance?

BERSERK: En maskert anti-kapitalist sparker inn et vindu i en butikk i Genovas gater.

sans recriminative
"special glove"

feel out
the state
of aesthetic

thingies—

("with a little string tied around it
but with a little *attachment*
twirled
kinda—
sorta—
over a triple
slip
knot
bow,
see? ")

From The Arctic Circle to Tierra del Fuego

* 9 syllables
* 126,000 miles
* 34 governmental compacts

e pluribus unum

FTAA

Constabulatory
Reverberative
Structualist
Limits?

Admirers?
or Northern Admiralties
patrolling the Hemispheres 'cross' 'cut' 'surface'
coasts

But to return to the *wessies* for a bit

If I write the way "the *mind* works," Athena, it's *Bellevue*

"sauvage!
hahven't you invehrted ourh mohneezimz
ccnohf?"

("do answehr")

It's that time of the year when my Anglo-American High
Modernist Dues

are due—

Strategy:

Secure second loan from the Multiversity Reach Out Bank
of America—

to pay off *interest* on
Amalgamated Langpo Support *Plank*—Bank

in order to make *first* payment on Chase
Global Goblins Bank of—

[splice in noun
radiative to de-slackened
labor market (*hmm*)]

Loan—

Whatever's left over, might (or might not) cover it

———

"code you
the squirly chimp—
and thus
monkey wrench (pre-programmatic) nutteries

on cue"

"An MLA

Cameo Camel's
public bent to
snort
'designate' 'specific' 'configuration' 'of' 'patronage' 'system'

on cue"

<habitus?>

sheetrock to plaster
flush—

"is this a *false* wall?
or a *real* wall?"

(knock knock
knock)

*

"Came we then to the place aforesaid by"

Bob Grenier [affix smiley face here] ☺

hand-sewn

3 copies, this is being No.2—

editions 1 and 3,

have a *grainier* look (in the main)

—in edition No. 3, the word "hocus"

appears as

"pocus" (but in supernal spaghetti font #7)

$120

(Canadienne)

*

"don' no*bah*dy—

'Brezhnev
-Era'
me"

*

lack of formal innovation
depth charges
starboard
cap'n

lack of historically sufficient depth

positioning
mein kapitan

dept
meter
dropping, mein—
droopy

aesthetic
integrity
is being
compromised!

<<alarm sounding>>

how not
das *butt*

how nut
twisted—

polydictory
liberatory
as unidididictory
horizon
dictum?

Mutatis Mutandis

"*who needs this*
'social movements' of the world
as world"

thingy"

a post priori

V.I.L.'s

sea lanes

(listservs)

patrolled

<habitus?>

*

Foucaultian
fitness walker
fulminating

"don' no*bah*dy!

don't *anyone*—

'Johnson
-Era'
me"

*

Affix
Fast Track
Authorization
Foreground
Decal

A friendly reminder from the Nachunal Poetry-Peanut Board's

point of production—
contractual—
patterned—
bargaining—
confederative—
american—
trade—

"u"

—guessed it—

[or hedged it, rather]

sectoral

twerker force

lateraturizations

in parallax

view—

trans-positioning

"run parallax now"

"2 years remaining—

for decrypter

'*satura*'

to

ins*crash*"

*

"Ducking the Décor;

or is it

Decorating the Ducking?"

(do answehr)

*

*sub*scene's
vest pocket
glossary

1st edition

what is:

"pot banging?"

*

Henry Rollins oracle,
sound as
tough turd always?

[counter pose with other period-marked singer

of inverted *affect*

from "other" primary
alimentary
ideolective

entry-point

multiplexed

"mouth"]

*

Volk—
Remunerative

STEINKASTING: Tildekte demonstranter kaster stein mot politiet.

Giuliani (the other, contemplexer) Carlo

CARLO!
Assonant

Cluster Chord

Abrazos—from here—still
For you

Omega

grl, boy—

the hat's on snug (always)—the paper one
—*over* my head—

Fugitive Crystal Shop (ground)

Banana Peel (figure)

Kid Marginal

(horse around)

Demo-Ready

Crashed—slain

Wasn't afraid of—*to*

"Fearful" Grid—

Dominant tone-relational—

(wink snort snort wink)

Capitalist Char-

—*all* the suturity

strictured

release?

(knock knock-

"albeit"

knock)

Megaportal—for

Frightful *and* Bountifully Fruitful

DEMOCRATIC TASKS

YET TO BE REALIZED

(1.) *Wahid.* Plug up three "originary" uni-directional <fixed> *orifices*—a hyper-individual activity

Ithnin. Manifest Worker Sabbaticals: 1 year off for every seven years worked (*happy*, to seal unemployment gap) [freedom of association right to collective bargaining right *axis*]

Thalata. Open up 6 <multi-directional> *artificial* Orifices (of no practical use *whatever*)—a hyper-massified activity

Arba'a. Realize Universal Health Care (cradle to grave)

Kamisa. Realize Equal Education (*flatten* tax base distribution)

Sitta. Cover up all newer orifices with another's surface—organelles—freely given—*by* them, becoming smooth & glowing—*every* pore's right to Feel Centrality, Being Equal (exchange)

Saba'a. MONSTROUS. Repeal Executive War Powers Act [task requires a MONSTROUS effort]

Thamania. Realize right to adequate housing & right to reproductive choice: as on the same plane, growth from the same nucleus—absolute-reaching out, porous ringlets sparkling, post-pleasure—plasmic

Tisa'a. 2000% increase for The Arts Funding

Ashara. (10.) 2000% increased understanding of: what can be spoken of as "aesthetic"

"Delete
All Barriers Now"

short cut—

("I don't see it
in this ordered mess
of yours
just now
moro")

recercare

"keep searching"

click, drag—drop
sinistro
one-half
centimeter (50 pixels left)

we'll take it!

(*that*—a

gain)

———

Ballooned
Incorporative
Psyche?

Globlalesco sin barreras

punctured subjects

gabby goblins

x'cuse me *cop a feels*—

"Politically Arrayed Poetics"

(designational—affective)

means—

miscalibrations

(no solamente
tranzas)

sizeable agglutables
sizeable non-agglutables

small *tokens*—

with * demands * (resin)

laced (constitutive)

oooffft

(conversation bubbly)

—ready?

blots

sacroiliac
rotates
diaphragm
de-contracts

mandible's

opening

up—

down—

simultaneous

dancing

blots—

"arcing"

* *MOTION* *

flared-out
in-
formational
forum
rousers

oomm pow take o
tip
turn

drig dro

spock shoo spoo
strak
froo

tg tg

tg

tsa—

at a tumbling
remembrance

somatic
roust about

release

oom
pow take o tip
turn

drig dro
dra

gru

sfooter
gru sfooter

rap built uptg

tf

tsh

tg tg tg

tssa—

Each
out-spacing-about
animate
social-contaminate
trip try a trapped troped code

past
"already social"
symboholic

sucksietal

bellies'

tribulations—

—Pot Banging!
—Pot Banging! *(cuz)*
—Pot Banging!

Agglutably
Argentinally
Yrs.—

demands—
ooofft

scalklers
out

(echo)

A Greater Americas

Resource Abundance *pulse*

Labor De-Deprivation *rhythm*

Ist kommen, mein—safado!
—just swung round the bend

"bing! bong!
BANG"

<soundy now>

oom
pow take o
tip
turn

drig

dro

shu
fa foh

Rib (doe di da—dib da)
Rib (di) (dib da)
Rib (da)

tg tg

Agglutibably
Port au Principally
Yrs.—

ooofft

hi ho!
In—

flared-out
trans
formational
rotary

fore*ground*
power-based
city-text
sfettered sectors

pectorally,
print—

—*vastus latoriously,* "vahrtual," *it's*

maximal gluteusly
MIND

—*at work*—

(*still*)

that *gone the way of another
expamperdenated national*

lip—eye—nose—

*trans-momied
native patch*

*blip blip
ka' blip*

jk' jk' jk'— ks'

—*at work*—

svectoring

flared-out
in-
trans-*sheeoeet*
formational

product

<this the axis?>

and NO product—

to belly
to belly
to belly

—*at NO* work—

<wahid> (1.)

emotional
gravitational
pull-ins

elasticky
way out

swung

elsewheres

lexicon

"ye shall know them by"

<ithnin>

content-rhythm

allo-imaginative

para-compassional

ranging

"on it"—
up—and

<*thalatha*>

getting

persistent

out visioning *in*

thorny

cousinly

horny

—**blogally**—

<*arba'a*>

spread out—

cozy

magnesium heart quicken

thicken the soup

poisoned

for them

password
for the New World?

<kamisa>

<u>no one has it</u>

and never—
never
more
under an
epistemic employ
of a

Homeland Security Patron

Ontologus—

vanquish

local native poet-chieftan's
boars (as in their wild pig
poesies)

transprosed you—
garlanded, ill-gauged

transversed you—

garlanded, ill-trans-positioned

a moment, a decade

arc velocity
differential
of

point-to-point

struggle

power

curve—

trip tro
drig dro

di

droped   tg tg

-tongue

tg

<sitta>

nix the
"between boundaries" (pomo-limbo)

incorporative
psych-like
thingy

rather,
slink through 'em—arc

around

for to

strample

um—

—solidarnosc (key)—

aporial tension

basis—

<saba'a>

"I listened
intently" [epitaph]

but
couldn't much—

but [epitaph]

lavished you

as never before [epitaph]
or since

openly [epitaph]

transitorily—

<*thamania*>

<*tisa'a*>

steadily—

<*ashara*> (10.)

De-Blot—

de-blot de-blot de-blot de-blot de-blot de-blot

¡¡¡*CASH SMAPITAL!!!*

oom
pow trake o
de-blot
trip
turn

drig
dro

de-blot
shu

FA

hhhh

eating cake

sssss—can't
n' spicy

globonesqueries

heats 'em up?

get *on up!*

you lexi

flexi

forms

at:

<u>Scene 2</u>

state date of reading—*nix* calendaric

false wall   reverb   marking

elser—

recercare

"I don't know *how*
she bore it—
but bore it
she did

tomorrow's

now"

trans-dis-equilibria

abrazos

omega

twerker force

Steinkasting

Omna ens habet aliquod esse propium

FLAMMEHAV

Group 4

Fourteen Superimposed Pockets of Formally Unified Subjectivity as Mass-Aggregate Social Subject, or, *Politesse Politique*, or, Monologue of the "Free Radical"

1.

"The problem's *TOO* big

2.

I—
might not be
appreciated!

3.

A millennium of oppression, and *no one*
put a halt to it

all—

4.

The millennium ahead, also absent of
my direct volition—

5.

doubtless, will remain the same (I can't know really—you're right, but)—it's an ill-fitting robe this thing of Conscious Response…if you don't mind, I'll—

6.

…there…

7.

oh, *this* funny undergarment here, it's

8.

Human Nature!

9.

un chien
mange un autre chien

(raaar)

* *

INTERLUDE

[a take off from Brecht]

The old woman off Broome Street
—at her alley's end
wielding a broom at loiterers
determined
to defend "it" (something)

constitutes
a
"movement"

* *

10.

"I'm not part of *any* movement I'm telling you"

11.

"What's more is, you're preaching to a convertible here"

12.

"you see, if mortality *itself* can't be conquered—what's the use?"

13.

Ya Vas lyubil tak iskrenno, tak nezhno

'I loved you earnestly, so tenderly'

—Pushkin

No pust' ona Vas bol'she nye trevoshit'

'But don't let it trouble you any further'

14.

(snug bubble-shaped shades—

head in the headwind—)

"puh-leeze!

dogmaticos—

leave me

be—

(inconspicuously)

free"

But Will Your Social Memory Cause Constipation Later in the Day? or That Something Else in the Morning?
paraphrasing a speech by
Pépé le <u>Rouge</u>

"Of all the postwar moments"

"Stalin, whose 'usefulness' Brecht had controversially acknowledged"

"The workers' protests in Poznan that June"

"A dress rehearsal, for the Hungarian Uprising in October"

"Within a month the death rattle of that imperial mission
of which Kipling was the bard"

"On the banks of the Suez Canal"

"Tovarich"

"The Left still had work to do <shocker>
but the Communist Party was not
up to it"

<nighty night>

"And this in turn
led first to the reorganization of the Left
<as cleft?—adrift?—bereft?>
in Western Europe, and then to
nineteen
sixty
eight"

<a settling-of-accounts, huh? does justice to...*itself*, huh?>

"And then the rise...
of the Women's Movement"

<of which you care little>

"And, from there,
the long and winding road to:
multiculturalism"

<anything else Mr. Clubfoot?>

"Then 'moral relativism' and Postmodernism"

Affekt Funereal / Affekt Jamboree
5-2001

(*as on TV*)

Welcome to this
special edition

double *cortege* for
Galbraith, Kenneth—
Friedman, Milton—

ssstately cortege...

efffusively-shiny
like your kids teeth—

...such *éclaircissement*
on this beautiful morning

lustrum
(kids, that's Latin, we mean to say
"wow")

...directly behind the caskets—is that
—it's the Macy's Rat (in mid-air)...neat, real neat...

in front
the lead-coated horses don't seem to mind the officers'
droppings...

is that a gigantic molar,
with worms popping out?
—such a *variety* of colors!

... look, some Teamsters
are in a tussle with some scab teletubby over on
23rd St. and Madison

...ok, now, now they're under arrest...

if you look carefully you'll see there's two *pre*-funeral exercises for
Fukuyama, Francis—
Soros, George—
on 24th

—not, not as stately...

a delegation of mainstream poets!

and behind them, this year's NPR security-clearance float!...ooh...

ya, they're rather new at this but...wait—

there's a lone guerrilla girl
running through the crowd now

she's

she's managed to get the Cultural Studies delegation
to strip and

dress up as

squeegee-bearing babushkas it looks like

...it's 20 degrees so, that's rather—ok, she's, she's
under arrest now...

...those are neat, those little plastic thingies, aren't they?...

The Bill Gates (My Charter) High School Marching Band!

The Steve Case (*My* Charter) High School Marching Band!

behind them
the post '89, post-historical
acrobat academics

on mini-lawnmowers...

that's smart...

The Yucky's!

The Yucky's, yeah, they're an interesting group...
they do things like suppress that
Sidney Poitier
is the best American actor *ever*

...oh look, the Fahd ibn Abdel Aziz al-Saúd
float

...the F14's behind him are real

...now, *that's* smart!

...I think he just waved at me

...who's that man with the Monocle grabbing his—

that's Mister Modernist!

he's been a regular at these events for over 90 years now

...Saga of The Blank Page float
a *real* favorite...

ooh, he just dropped his—wait

a babushka—her, her boot's—

crkkkk....

oh, that's, that's not good...but

—did you know that

these are the first
100% soy
caskets
ever made?

some people have actually run up to nibble at them...

kids, if you're watching this...

make sure you never think of any other social arrangement
other than one that

Militarily Has To Dominate Three Quarters of The World

Ideo-Degradable Verses from Immokalee
(for Lucas Benitez)

> *"but to tell of the other things I saw there"*
> —Dante's *Inferno*, Book One.

"In the Everglades—
In the Tomato Industry— "

Are you *yourself?*

"Actually, I'm *not* a tomahto
(any more than you are, at least)"

"The day
starts us at 4:00 am"

"The 'grew leethas'
(que es eso?)
grew leethas...(o!
crew leaders!)
exacto!"

"They pick us—
up on a truck—and take us
to the performance site"

"Till sundown"

"45 cents a bucket"

"Fields sometimes been picked twice or even three times before getting there"

"Buckets weigh 35 pounds"

("am I boring you?")

(actually, yes, you are, at this point,
I'm in need of some
torque-age)

(bueno, eso lo tenemos, vea aqui)

"We haul them some 100 feet to the trucks
some 200 hundred times"

"They don't whisper gentle ayres into our ears—*not to*
 (one after the other) miss a single tomato
                                         (instanter)"

And about the slavery rings?

"Oh, folks from Mexico and Guatemala brought up and
 not allowed to move around
at will— "

"Permission to go to the store granted, maybe, but the guards go
with them"

"$100 a week; and from that, $60 for 'service charges'
(for 'the passage')
an additional 15 for 'rent'"

"Leaves
$25 a week— "

Taco Bell

(could you please tweak or twaddle that, now, a little, for me)

"if you *must*
have it"

"Wacko Bull"   "Bucko Ghoul"

(*what?*)

("calmado, compañero, concentrese, absorba
esta intervención")

"…is the primary consumer of the product produced
(not the *secondary* consumer of the product produced,
$$\textit{you})"$$

How much
would they have to increase
the price of a 99 cent product?

"How price they much to have increase of product 99 cents?"

"Would you prefer that in Luther's German, The King's English,
or Harvard School of *Latifundista* Spanish?"

State it kingly

"*One-tenth of one cent*"

"Add that public money (State and Federal) goes to the growers
to fund (*and* subsidize) them
for on-going *public* research into
Improved Growing Methods"

"And it confronts us, hermano,
immediately and everyday
our status, the barrier of
no documents
dogs us"

"We can't participate
more openly
in politics
(let alone…)"

"So that the question of amnesty
is primary"

Anything else you'd like to say, Lucas?

"Yeah,

—we're workers too! With special problems and solutions to those problems. We need help from all sorts of people. *Boycott Taco Hell.* I'd like to send warm greetings to all of our brother and sister workers

wherever they may be"

Jukebox Selection,
a Brick and Mortar Remembrance
following a conversation with a Local 4-121 pensioner

How did widget make you feel about marriage?

How did marriage make you feel about widget?

How did you make widget feel
about widget?

And how did it react?

And how
to your extra-widgetory
gallivanting?

And widget wanted children
at about
that time.

How much *did* widget resent
your harboring feelings for
(your uneasy reveries of)
The Curved Plow—

Widget read you bed-time stories:
Pluckboy, Punthouse, Wrustler.

It was

a hoppin'
sexcapade—everyone all greased up
nitrous cellutone
packaged widgetings
panting
credit
sirening.

But, you widgeted yourself (praise be) to a series of regular Sunday morning

Services—

Yr. son's liberal widgetry department
deserved, no, was destined for:
a make-over, but around a different
social axis (a near finite set of substantive pointer nouns)

But
not
just
yet—

Not yet.

Fad diets
and dominatrixes
began stalking him (simultaneously)

Cut down on
Widget

Increase
Widget

Tell widget you want
firm widgetings.

As there *was* a widget inside him
waiting to come out.

His
Inner-Widget
told him so.

No,
nor will *I* ever
hear the word widget
without thinking of
—*y'alls*—

particular

rock n' roll

"fantasy"

Die Warheit ist Konkret

the waiter,
had till that time engaged us only on a rather cursory level of
what do you (two) do
and this in an exceedingly tranquil manner
and it was done repeatedly
and was always forgotten, and so was asked over and over
and over, to the point of exhaustion which, for him, turned out
to be the freshest of
vantage points from which
to launch –
                he went

                      Falun Gong

        on our ass

right there, right before us leaving The Bay Area

"master Li" said he, "thinking of what I'm thinking about
– right now – but, on another time-plane...
many universes...happening   our body... is *change*

I'm never so ha' ha' happy"

trembling now – agitated as he was, a tumescence that was – is,
unmistakably, *programmatic*, and after clearing away our salty
Spinach Soup, "Hillary C, (as in the upper case letter C) you

going to vote for when you get there right?"

I miss that damn restaurant mainly for its Vegetarian Beef with
Black Bean Sauce with those
big ol' (unapologetic) Onions
          and
picking up a copy of the People's Daily World from a nearby
vending machine on the way there
          and
nibbling on it before ordering, which had some needed morsels
of nutrition (reports of goings-on) but was for the most part
devoid of any viewpoint or analysis that used or even
approached as its axis-of-intervention the principal of

> *l'émancipation des travailleurs sera l'oeuvre*
> *des travailleurs eux-mêmes*

said here in French so as to annoy English, so as to broach it in
the original German, spiking it (if I could've, better then, than
now) in Mandarin, Spanish being reserved for this more local-
ized determining instance of – rebuke – *you know who you* –
intimidator of immigrant waiters, re:

ALIGNMENT: *se ve – se siente? o es, simplemente?*

many universes
other time-planes

        is changed
        the body?

the stalinoid CCP
goes around arresting people for even having publicly done the
"centering" mind-body *excor*cises, however impartially performed

many of the Top Cats (black, white, or checkered) of the "**FG**"
are well ensconced in the **RS**, Railway Secretariat (or industry)
as well as some in the **MS**, Mining Secretariat (or industry)

they are not well –

though the light manufacturing (independent-union crushing)
Tiggers in the SEZ's
are quite well –

good (bad) cadres
      vs.
bad (good) cadres

Mon, why seestu love and herte
On worldes blisse that nout ne last?

Thu lickest huny of thorne, iwiss,
That seest thy love on worldes bliss
For full of biterness it is

Some Brooklyn Northside *Calaveritas* (Little Skulls) (Ironic Morsels)

Suppose
pondering the cultural flock
some high noon

mock sacrificial
metallurgic offering—

to recuse
himself
arrivismo?

subjective
transference

"chosen"

Into a pit

pleasant paranoia
peaceful

feeling—

A break from
prolet-kampf
agonistics?

Blows up
in a materialite-speckled
face

Hungering
resist
two specialties

Content and its

porns

History not as something
you can live to tell your children

whispering

a tin heart—
a silver stomach—
(a steel-tempered—
into a chrome-plated—)

get youself
with someone else *alloy*
and forge

a borg-like
transference

a real estate
shake out
snatch up

a Lazarus come back from
graduate studies

sarcasmic
mock ecstatic

"please!"
(in polish)
proszę

Acclimate?

frightening how fast
rousted

from The Southside
Boriquas

"fuckin' bummed out, dude, just—"

chasing the creamer?

Silicon pilgrims conferring
(as ever)

On the runway
Bedford L-stop
prima donut
silver
diablo
vivora

adjective
blizzard

live / wack (off)
space conversion

beezulhubbub "nifty" guy
goofbar—

$4.50
a pint!

Kurva!

americanium
[that's a real element by the way]
americanium
-plated
buns!

carbo's—
into super
buggery insulin-spiking

conversion

a Iago-like
"wacky wit"
follows

an art-fart
come out

the mouth
poesy

an anarcho
-*what-have-you-ist*
slides into
dapper doubt—

after Nader

*

titanium birds chirping

(makes this an installation thing)

*

static

from the vibrant

lebensraum

lofts

*

we are chosen

*

transference

*

recused?

yes!

I am *not* of

said subcults of weird

displaced

(offset)

politics

*

(or am I?)

*

stress like *that*

*

squeezing out
alu-mi-ni-um
doodad
happiness

*

Trotsky: how'd you *get* here?

Me: how'd *you* get here?

Group 5

About the Amadou Diallo Police Shooting, a Verse Letter to T. G.
1-28-2000

yesterday (Sunday) we finally did hook up with the march down Broadway

No Justice?
No Peace!

towards
(historically)
what end?

a criminal re-trial? *unlikely.*

a civil court trial—*possible*, and?

once begun (energies going there)
as footnote in the affair?

they did: a crime: the cops—
what "criminal" statutes, are cops held to?

and so can we talk about it—Power

there's Minimalist and Maximalist political demands
(attentive to dynamics of the moment)

to not (from the jump) *comp* to
monistic impulse
the whole tamale
"revolution"

what matters the radical flavor of the rhetoric?
(*rheto*r, be still, for a moment)

...are you
for something like:
an Independent Community Review Board of the police?
(ICRB)

ability to hire and fire, approve or reject "programs" carried out by precincts—

checking The Department's agency—self-validating authority 100% hegemonic

a something beyond
"(just) Fuck Tha Pigs"
prurience

and so, what *demand*

pursue to

concretize

and how would such a board be constituted?
appointed by same villains?

or elected—accountable

a composite of the population corresponding to the population being "policed"

our civil liberties defended?
yes, but what's more: transformed

lutta continua

and so the slogan:
all cops out of our neighborhoods—now! (period)

the *affect*
though justified

yet, is it
already (in any way) a mass
political demand?

working class of the Burroughs stand ready to—ouster?

8 or 9 folks, down Broadway, one "a wigger" (blonde dreads) pitching that, lively *rhetors*, spirited components of the march, that from the hip shoot—straight?

the task of The Moment
not some form of ICRB?

U.S. working class (especially Black, Latino) fight for it repeatedly—every function of the Bourgeois State, opposes—

and a longer discussion (later), this next—
that
U.S. has not had viable mass working class party

since Debs Socialist Party

to push for such a Thing, do you?

if so,

what current efforts / parties now include ICRB's in platform

to counter
the *countless*
"operations"

"apache" "viper" "moonlight prairie fire"

conjured up by
countless
RepubliCratic "mandates"

roll populations, *shake-out*

The Bronx, 6 years Stop-and-Frisk "Operation"
(code-named, I forgot frontier-sounding jingle)

no probable charge whatsoever—required

"mutual relations...are degrading daily"
quoth He, anchorchimp, on TV—

though state of "warfare"
is *unilateral!*

organized

......
......

And the march (having
begun at the United Nations)
—we caught up with it at around 16th
all the way down to City Hall—some 2 hrs—3 cops to every
non-cop...

but you say
why not do away
with police *altogether*?

ok!
end-goal, yet

police are Alpha and Omega of system itself—last guardians
(with armed forces)

would be: The Eve
of Revolution
itself

literal abolishment of State Apparatus

[my ostensibly Leninist outlook]

so, what is The Demand?
(transitional <minimalist> demand)

as we were down there at City Hall, on knees, wallets raised
(previous to such an "Eve")

No Justice?
No Peace!

mean we to: *encroach, or not?* on Right that State reserves
(exclusively) for itself?

as form—beyond
solely "outraged"—demonstrably so
(as who couldn't be? Nazi-like NYPD!)

as form—beyond
non-contestation of civic terrain
—pre-ICRB (status quo), "moral appeal," in the main—

but with "revolutionary" patina?
then *that*

more truly
(quote) "rearguard reformism"

re: the (ultra-leftist) charge

inverted
redirected

back at cha' (preemptive even!)
actually chuckling now—at it (and at myself), Ted—

but so that we can talk about it (no frills)—Power—

as form—

from content

yrs,
as ever,

RT

Blue-Green Superfund Roundelay

Perma-*Laboro*-Centristic
breaks bread with
Enviro-Mass-Reductio
cautiously
creatively-tense

parvenue
alliance
Verfremdungseffekt
theater
"familiarly-alien"

effects
trip
the unconverted
crude
oil
derivatives
laity

geist

diesel
ethanol
methanol
fall

on the third day rise

spiffy?

for coal's sake,
stick to it?

Internal Combustion's
aesthetic
campaigns

From intake stroke to exhaust stroke
UTILITARIAN
scaffolding

"we can't just
use it?"

A Questionable Account of *Ancient*-Future Life

The Works and Days
Ascribed to
AMOCO

pre-classical
paradigms
unstable
about to blow

post-particulate standards
counter-consensus
process

Spirit of Karen Silkwood

infusion

Spirit of *comités*
populares
tri-national
borders
cleanup

Phantoms of Kyoto Accords
suffusion

solar, wind, hydrogen

—*usefully*—
COUNTER-UTILITARIAN

syncretic-to-synergetic

concentrates

counter-campaign's
conversions

towards?

A JUST

TRANSITION

.

A Postscript

On related plane
to contrast previous
oppositional formation's
specificity

Workers to demand "Independent Community Review Board"
for their affairs?

hell no!

Workers self-representation
in relation to immediate employers'
"needs," incontrovertibility of interests (at optimal)
imbedded *in* the demands

This "potentiality"

With both minimalist and maximalist aspects
if realized, ie. a strike—

Minimalist as
Re-Appropriation of Surplus *itself*—at point-of-production

(over "contract"—specific social form, in *our* time)

Maximalist as
organizational
expansion of horizon of self-representation

Toe-to-Toe

"Terretorialization"

Counter-hegemonic

Proto-Hegemon—The Worker's Council

Assemblies of 'em

Socialism, pre- 1929 32 and 36 plenary re-writings of
Soviet Constitution
codification of devolution of worker's democracy—

Through Party's Courts
Cheka's and Army's
complete jurisdiction over 'em

Working atoms of socialism

"Independent" *of* extrinsic legislation, though interlinked—
and radiating culturally *outward*

Forms

General Secretary Lula's Last Stand?
(A verse letter to SW, on the heels of a wave of regional strikes in Brazil)

> "General Secretary
> Lula's
> Last?"

who stood
at the previous PT convention
bewildered amidst the scramble of

>> silver spurred
>> ascendant
>> lieutenants

who were neither assured of, nor sure of their motion's directions nor suffering

> the resulting splits

effectively hamstrung
the mystique
of the media-popular
General Secretary

                by prefacing all motions to the floor
                "popular committees' wishes being..."

(meanwhile their respective regional bases
                                      lay fallow)

(deep in-roads by the right detected
popularly
in the spring)

So not "Contra-Lula" plots (and subplots, the fibers
of your gossipy prose
analysis)

but Trans-Lula-Distinctive
currents (with about 5 separate trends

and an average of
two tendencies within each)

                all the while a pressure / need to consolidate
                against said inroads
                felt by those
                close to "base" / *being* base
                (elected local worker-peasant)
                delegates

were in the background
at the convention
as in a mural
motionless

        and of the 3 dominant currents
        all 3 ostensibly
        neo-liberal!

as per critique developed by
O Trabalho (fraternal section of the ILC)

that did win several key principalities
this summer in
Porto Alegre, Recife, and smaller *favelas* in the Mato Grosso

And stands (the OT) against IMF payments on interest
(*or* principal, same, tail-eating dragon)

a "bomba economica" that, comrade Messina summed up so well

in San Francisco, to the great approval of the SF Labor Council
(which has been drifting to the left for years now, substantively)

but, here also, can the OT PT *congresistas*

speak from a mobilized base?

My only point I suppose is this:

> *A pox on* Lula! (the man)
> (despite the dedicated work he's done)

The Tragedy of Lula, Prince of the PT

if presently,
the social bases
are too detached from its Representational Apparatus

isn't that the Tragedy of the Moment?

———

Written 5 29-2001. Author's position in the summer of 2002 was "All out for Lula!" in the coming November elections.

Notes on the Great Strike of '97

A move (at last)

                        a move
                        meant

Defrocked

            is happenstance

                            The usual grievance procedures
                            long gone

Incontrovertibility of the positions
become plain

                            Tens of thousands
                            Arraigned—is
                            one way to put it

Beholden to?

            The burden of proof
            on us
            ok

                            In the wake of
                            so many
                            asynchronous stabs at

Regroupment

Hash out—
lock in—
the action-plan

                        (synchronous)

—Strike!

                        As for
                        the abrogation
                        of past settlements
                        (that is, truces)

Pleasure-pain of
every passing hour

            Relish

Not flimsidarity
(the socio-sexuality of the ruling class is flimsidarity)

                        As "in it
                        for the long haul"

Preponderance of confidence
building

                (these emotions—de-skilled as they've been
                can attest?)

                                        Retaliatory (to the core)
                                        unapologetically
                                        the front—broadens

"let's go—see
how we figure
into it"

                                        A measurable cut *into*
                                        disaffectedness
                                        institutional
                                        disaffectedness

(that was "experimental", pups
this might or might not be)

                                        Henceforward—
                                        a sense of entitlement
                                        (as yet unofficial)

Carved out collectively

Collaterally rousing—others

                                        "can I join in
                                        in it?"
                                            who were
                                            (and this advisedly)
                                            "free" to

On the victorious nation-wide Teamsters strike against UPS.

And Yet Another Incipient Form or Face, Venal "Left" Cooptative Rump of the WTO, NGO-ite Operative's Proclamation—Baldly—Put

(quoting)

"In Brazil, WE
        have
                a movement, that is
                    particularly
                          eloquent
in showing
        potentialities
            for
                Cultural
                      Change
forged
by
CIVIC SOCIETY
                      itself
around the ISSUE of
                    social exclusion
                          -*ism*
IT
has
        a UNIVERSAL
        dimension
despite
its
        unique Brazilian

                        features
After all
[*after all*
 —after all]
            IT
              appeals
to
CITIZEN'S
          consciousness

the
movement
is
a
LEARNING
                process
for
the
       citizenry

based
on
        ethical
            INDIGNATION

the
movement
              directs
                    ITSELF
to those
      integrated

in
the current
       development
model
                        to ENABLE
    them

to see
OTHER'S
       and
       assume
               responsibility
as
citizens
      for
      their
           FATE"

* * *

The Dane
with disdain
for the peasant's recalcitrance
      for their organization's
      dissolving
      into

the
"movement"
           headquartered
           in Brussels

                    headed by the
                    Schroederesque—"third way"-ist
                            anschluss
                                        louse

            who
            has discovered
            homo pluralisticus

for democratic
                vistas...

                        is offended
                        (the Dane)

[by them self-organized trade unions too]

/// as to how come
                you

            and you
                        and you

have not LEARNED thee

        the

rrr...RRR...*radical*
                            break
from the "bi-
polar

      political"
      past
            into that

  rrr...ludic
            p r o j e c t

* * *

us

"masternarrativists"

            "economists"

"idealists"

            "workerists"

"statists"

            "essentialists"

ortho- gap-toothed
            foos

Hidden Harvest

from a distance
almost festive

rippling in the morning breeze

soft conversations
great piles of scallions

a pungent sun illuminates the faces of young girls

she keeps grabbing them, straightening out their roots and tails

in a little gesture of self-consciousness, she pulls her sweater
away from her face
knocks the dirt off, ties a rubber band around them

Ejido San Quintin

all are packed in ice
and shipped to Great Britain

———

from a distance
almost restive

rising to the 20th floor

clipped conversations
great piles of papers

a humming fax machine illuminates the faces of young girls

they keep grabbing at her, straightening out her hands and fingers

in a little gesture of self-consciousness, she pulls her sweater away from her face
lifts it off the paper tray, sticks a sticky on it

Ejido San Quintin

all are packed in ice
and shipped to Great Britain

---

from a distance
almost resistive

basking in the building's fluorescent light

algebraic conversations
great piles of direct objects

a deadened emotion illuminates the faces of young girls

he keeps changing them, sorting out the nouns and verbs

in a little gesture of trained-consciousness, he quickly minimizes the screen from his face
knocks the dirt off, ties a rubber band around them

Ejido San Quintin

all are packed in ice
and shipped to Great Britain

———

from a distance
almost imperceptive

breezing through the morning frequencies

anxious reservations
great piles of diners

a poetry audience illuminates the faces of young girls

she keeps grabbing them, straightening out their roots and social whereabouts

in a non-literal gesture of class-consciousness, he pulls her sweater away from her face
knocks the dirt off, ties a rubber band around them

Ejido San Quintin

all are packed in ice
and shipped to Great Britain

---

from a distance
almost assertive

shuffling through the evening news

moot conversations
great piles of rotting vegetables

a pungent spin-off literature illuminates the faces of young girls

it keeps grabbing him, chopping up his roots and raison d'êtres

in a tactically abstract solidarizing gesture of class-consciousness,
she peels his self-conscious piece away from her face

knocks the dirt off, ties a rubber band around it

Ejido San Quintin

all are packed in ice
and shipped to Great Britain

Ejido: A landholding community owned collectively by its members. In 1992, the Mexican congress (largely at the behest of Wall Street) passed legislation aimed at watering-down Article 27 of the Mexican Constitution (guaranteeing the fundamental economic and cultural rights of the ejidos), opening the way for the privatization and commercialization of the lands, thus rendering the peasants' political gains (stemming from the Mexican Revolution of 1910-1917) effectively moot.

Some Thoughts on the Upcoming Quebec Summit, or Fractals from the I-Experience Colliding with the We-Experience, Utterances

The sewer entrances have been sealed
lest we
reach the city's center

Orsainville has been emptied of its 600 inmates
to make room for us

We still outnumber the bastards
200 to 1

*

Breaching the security perimeter

for a moment
to link arms

(brushes, drums,
pens)

to face tear gas and truncheons

trust

the vinegar-soaking doo-rag
girl

beside you—

in the clutch

(but "trust"
a poem?

—that's plain batty!)

*

For Voloshinov, reported speech is
"utterance within utterance,
utterance about utterance"

"a generative process can only be grasped
by way of another one"

ol' Volosh—

in the clutch

as to how much

might be refracted

from an "event"

(in advance even!)

the no-show or participant
persons
those

(these)

the no-show or participant
piece or matrix
this

for a moment

*la convergence
des forces*

"tear gas" "pens" "utterances" "trust" "the bastards" "face"
"doo rags" "link" "you" "arms" "girl" "face" "trust"
"vinegar-soaking" "utterances" "arms" "utterances" "pens" "we"?

"face" "you"?
"links" "trust" "truncheons" "the bastards" "pens"?

"links" "trust"
to "trust"?

"truncheons"
"trust"?

"breaching
the security perimeter"

"drums!"

…no
"real"
shutdowns
here

but a series
of standoffs

before a standoff

Atelos was founded in 1995 as a project of Hip's Road and is devoted to publishing, under the sign of poetry, writing that challenges the conventional definitions of poetry, since such definitions have tended to isolate poetry from intellectual life, arrest its development, and curtail its impact.

All the works published as part of the Atelos project are commissioned specifically for it, and each is involved in some way with crossing traditional genre boundaries, including, for example, those that would separate theory from practice, poetry from prose, essay from drama, the visual image from the verbal, the literary from the non-literary, and so forth.

The Atelos project when complete will consist of 50 volumes.

The project directors and editors are Lyn Hejinian and Travis Ortiz. The director for text production and design is Travis Ortiz; the director for cover production and design is Ree Katrak.

Atelos (current volumes):

1. *The Literal World*, by Jean Day
2. *Bad History*, by Barrett Watten
3. *True*, by Rae Armantrout
4. *Pamela: A Novel*, by Pamela Lu
5. *Cable Factory 20*, by Lytle Shaw
6. *R-hu*, by Leslie Scalapino
7. *Verisimilitude*, by Hung Q. Tu
8. *Alien Tatters*, by Clark Coolidge
9. *Forthcoming*, by Jalal Toufic
10. *Gardener of Stars*, by Carla Harryman
11. *lighthouse*, by M. Mara-Ann

12. *Some Vague Wife*, by Kathy Lou Schultz
13. *The Crave*, by Kit Robinson
14. *Fashionable Noise*, by Brian Kim Stefans
15. *Platform*, by Rodrigo Toscano

Distributed by:

Small Press Distribution	Atelos
1341 Seventh Street	P O Box 5814
Berkeley, California	Berkeley, California
94710-1403	94705-0814

to order from SPD call 510-524-1668 or toll-free 800-869-7553
fax orders to: 510-524-0852
order via e-mail at: orders@spdbooks.org
order online from: www.spdbooks.org

The author's e-mail address is RT5LE9@aol.com

Platform
was printed in an edition of 1,000 copies
at Thomson-Shore, Inc.
The cover was printed at Southeastern Printing.
Text design and typesetting by Lyn Hejinian and Travis Ortiz
using the Adobe version of the classic typeface
Garamond for the text and GillSans for the titles.
Cover design by Dirk Rowntree.